SEASONS

JUDY COLE

Grosvenor House
Publishing Limited

The right of Judy Cole to be identified as the author of this
work has been asserted in accordance with Section 78
of the Copyright, Designs and Patents Act 1988

The book cover is copyright to Judy Cole
Cover photo ©www.istockphoto.com/gb/portfolio/maxiphoto

This book is published by
Grosvenor House Publishing Ltd
Link House
140 The Broadway, Tolworth, Surrey, KT6 7HT.
www.grosvenorhousepublishing.co.uk

This book is a work of fiction. Any resemblance to
people or events, past or present, is purely coincidental.

A CIP record for this book
is available from the British Library

ISBN 978-1-78623-631-9

For Sandra

CONTENTS

INTRODUCTION

Our walk with the Lord is a continuous season of prayer.

Within that season are many others. Our God speaks to us of His love and glory through all of them.

May my experience of these seasons of prayer find an echo, and be an encouragement, in your own.

THE
PRAYER
SEASON

Prayer Prepares

Prayer soaks the dry ground
Prayer is rain
It is water, the water of tears
Softening and melting hard hearts
Raising a fragrance from parched fields

Without prayer, seeds do not take root
Fruit does not grow
In our lives, in our circumstances, in our land

Pray, so the soil may be prepared
The ground expectant
For the harvest

Companionship

Prayer
A time of companionship
A dialogue
A wordless exchange of thought and desire

Prayer

Drawing from me love and worship
Tears and joy

Prayer

Drawing from Him
Grace, compassion, and strength

Prayer

Pray

In prayer, seeds are sown
Flowers bud, fruit ripens
Nothing visible for man to see
But within
The earth of souls is tilled
In due season there is a great harvest

Pray

In prayer, the flesh is starved
But the heart is fed
The tears of the broken-hearted are known and
captured
Holy joy fills empty lives
Strength is renewed
Pray

Prayer From The Heart

Prayer from the heart prepares me to hear
Opens me, softens me
Breaks me, silences me
Prayer from the heart turns me towards
my Father's face
Fills me with Jesus

Prayer

God's means of communication
God's gift

The Nature Of Prayer

I do not pray to make myself comfortable
I approach Father through prayer with fear and
trembling
Because that for which I have asked He will answer

Prayer, true prayer costs
It demands all I have
That I relinquish all I am
Prayer is an emptying and a filling
Prayer is entering into the timelessness, the
spaciousness of God
Prayer is my lifeblood and my breath

Prayer is risky
Prayer is fulfilling
Prayer helps me to stand firm
For the times when the rains don't fall
And my land is a desert

Prayer helps me to see and to hear
Sometimes amazing me
Often confounding me
Always drawing me deeper into Him
In love, in faith, in wonder

The Effect Of Prayer

Prayer establishes my foundations
Prayer brings structure to the scatterings of my life
Prayer permeates and directs my ways
Prayer sharpens my view, brings the way into focus
Prayer takes me from insecurity
To a place of safety
In the arms of my Lord

Prayer Warfare

It is a vast battleground
This battleground of deception
That seeks to separate the soul from its resting place
in Christ,
As sons of our Father

This is a battle waged and won through prayer
The prayer of faith
That brings victory in slight skirmish, in mighty
onslaught

Through prayer, vision is restored
Mountains are moved
Hope is renewed
The enemy retreats
The Kingdom advances

There is but one place that remains constant
The Cross
Where the soul kneels
Praying

Join with me in the warfare of prayer

Praying In The Kingdom

Praying
Praying for the people
Proclaiming the Kingdom
The rule that has begun
Blessing homes with the truth of salvation

Praying
Praying for the people
Release of the prisoners
Praying in God's authority
God's majesty
God's justice

Praying
Speaking out the Name above all other names
For dulled hearts and aching souls to hear
For the silent dead to awake
Releasing the aroma of Christ's saving grace

A Prayer for God's Light

I look at the street lights
Sending out small pools of light

Street lights are good
We need them in the night
But they are not the real thing

I pray we will never settle for lamp light that goes out
at the rising of the sun
The lamp light of our own projects, desires and
achievements

I pray for the radiance of God to shine in our land
That shining glory that puts out all other lights

I pray we will be looking for the dawn of our Lord's
coming,
His Kingdom
That we will be ready and waiting

A Prayer For The Wind

Come and visit us again, Wind of the Spirit
Shake us out of the trees of our complacency and
comfort

Wind of the Spirit
The Spirit of Jesus
Blow the dust from our minds
The apathy from our hearts
Forgive us when weariness saps our zeal

Wind of the Spirit
Stir us, thrill us
So that we are left longing for more
Desirous of nothing less

Blow with Your Wind on every group and gathering
Dialogue and decision
Telephone, text and tweet
Meeting and ministry

Blow with fire upon every heart
Old in faith, young in faith
Frail in body, sick in mind, weary in heart

Blow with the Wind of Your Spirit
Blow us off our feet
Off the ground which has become our anchor
Blow
Shake up all we are
All we do, all we have
Blow with the whirlwind of Your Presence
So that it is all You, all You are, and all You do
We need You

A Prayer For Healing

I pray the Lord will revive and restore our vision of
Him
Our God, the Great Healer

Forgive us Father, our tired, helpless hearts
Forgive us for when we minimise and rationalise
Your power to heal
I pray we may again see mighty miracles of
restoration

I pray for those who live under a great weight
The weight of uncertainty of ill health and its effect
Let there be a release from the fear of pain, of doctors,
of change, of the future
May there be a lifting of the cloud of anxiety and grief
And a rising of faith
Give us visions of hope, and the constancy of Your
love
Make known to us Your loving compassionate heart
You who bore, and still bear our sickness on that vile
Cross
Make this our anthem as we cry out to You in trust, in
love, in adoration

THE
SEASON OF
MEDITATION

Reflecting on Scripture

Lord, Our Lord
How Majestic Is Your Name In
All The Earth!
(Psalm 8:1)

His majestic name fills the earth
Supreme
Lord of all
Filling mind, body, soul

Illuminating the way
Silencing foes
Calming fears
Heightening joy

His majestic name releases troubled hearts
Oils wounds
Cleanses wrongdoing
Rules
Triumphant and victorious

His majestic name is the answer to man's deepest
question
Dispelling evil's odour
Delivering life's fragrance
Filling all things
His majestic name
Jesus

He Reveals The Deep Things
Of Darkness
And Brings Utter Darkness Into
The Light
(Job 12:22)

I have pierced the darkness
The darkness of your disbelief and disobedience
I have pierced the darkness with My light
The light of salvation in the name of My Son
The light of deliverance from all that held you captive

I have pierced your darkness with My light
Don't shut your eyes against its brilliance
Don't allow it to be talked away, explained away,
stolon away
Don't allow time or circumstance or idols to darken
the light

You see it, you know it, you have tasted its glory
Now love it, live in it, believe in it
I have pierced your darkness
Give Me the glory

"Then Jesus Declared, 'I Am The Bread Of Life. Whoever Comes To Me Will Never Go Hungry, And Whoever Believes In Me Will Never Be Thirsty." (John 6:35)

Dear Love
I am like the deer
Chasing through the forest
Startled…
I have been pierced by Your darts
I am transfixed, overcome
The beauty of Your love breaks me
I raise my eyes to Your glory
Healing love flows

Bread of Life, Bread of Life
I dare to draw near
Rest my head on Your heart
I feed, I drink, I live
Intoxicated by Your presence
Your passion, Your power, Your love

Bread of Life, Bread of Life
Fill me more
Till I am satiated, overflowing
Yet fill me more
I cling to You
Desiring nothing else
Knowing nothing else
Understanding nothing else
Only that You are the only Bread that can satisfy

"My Father, If It Is Not Possible For This Cup To Be Taken Away Unless I Drink It, May Your Will Be Done"
(Matthew 26:39)

I tip the cup upside down
No dreg, no drop remains
It was heavy and brim-full
The cup of the Lord's righteous judgement
But now it lies empty

I hold it
Weightless in my hand
An object without purpose
A vessel devoid of use for it has no content
It can be put aside
A passing memory, forgotten

And the bitter brew that once fermented within?
What of that portion that awaited me?
It has been drunk and consumed
Willingly, lovingly, entirely

By the only One worthy who could ever drink it and
live again
My punishment has been paid
My life has been bought
By Jesus

Rejoice my soul
Lay aside your sadness
See the Lamb
See His scars
Death's cup lies empty
Jesus lives again

"Stand At The Crossroads And Look, Ask For The Ancient Paths, Ask Where The Good Way Is, And Walk In It, And You Will Find Rest For Your Souls" (Jeremiah 6:16)

Bind me to You
Impress me on Your heart
My Lover, my Lord
Fill my empty heart

Bind me to You
That wherever I go
I may bring the power of Your Presence
The fragrance of Your Presence
Even the offence of Your Presence

Bind me to You that what You bear
I may bear also
When You are afflicted
So too am I afflicted
Only bind me to You

May Your wounds be mine
Your ridicule mine
Though it cut me mightily
It is nothing compared to being bound to You
Rejoicing in the joy You bring
Hidden in You
Held by You
Your ways are mine
Daily You reveal them to me
They are good

"... I Will Awaken The Dawn" (Psalm 57:8)

I will wake the dawn with my song
I will bring His day into my night
I will welcome His sunlight into my soul's
wanderings
I will do this
I will declare He is Sovereign
I will praise my beloved Lamb

I will wake the dawn with my song
I will do this

All that seeks to woo me into a poisonous embrace
Of idols and false gods
Of despair and dread
Will disappear
For they are of the night
And I am of His day

I will wake the dawn with my song
In the Lord alone will I rejoice

"The God Of Heaven Will Give Us Success. We His Servants Will Start Rebuilding ...." (Nehemiah 2:20)

Jesus, my Saviour and Deliverer has come
Dragons seek to deceive and to accuse
To bind and to muzzle

But Jesus has come to rebuild my walls
And He wants me to take part in my restoration
Jesus has come to tell me of how it was in Eden
How it is now, and how it will be in Paradise

Jesus has come, for His heart was broken
Broken over my brokenness
He has come to carry away the burden of sin
The rubble of guilt and shame

Jesus has come and He is not going away again
In His coming He has brought hope and life
Demons tremble
The walls are rising
Jesus has come

"Blessed Is He Who Comes In The Name Of The Lord" (Mark 11:9)

It's easy to join in the celebration of the King of Kings
Surrounded by family, friends, fine music, sunshine
and laughter
It's easy to bathe in the warmth of Jesus' beautiful
smile and gentle hands
Bringing healing, encouragement and love

It's hard to leave lovely Sunday
Walk into lonely Monday
Me and my Master
But it's why Jesus came

It's hard to allow Him freely into the silence of my
heart
To permit the Refiner's Fire to sear me
Illuminate those idols, those desires, cowering in dark
recesses
But it's why Jesus came

It's hard to come out from the crowd
To embrace the Cross
Confront the world's so-called moralities and
freedoms
Stand against all that offends the Holy Name
But it's why Jesus came

Oh God, I love it when we worship You together in
Spirit and Truth
But how much I love it
When You pierce the walls of the temple of my heart
When we walk out together
Proclaiming Your Kingdom
Engaging in warfare against a defeated foe

Lord, upturn the tables
Release the captives
Come, and come again

"For God Made Christ, Who Never Sinned, To Be The Offering For Our Sin, So That We Could Be Made Right With God Through Christ"
(2 Corinthians 5:21)

Punishment gone
Guilt washed away
Angels singing
Saints dancing
It is finished
Incomparable God

Too much
Too much to take in
But enough
More than enough
In which to rejoice

No more excuses not to praise
No more penance to pay
No problem too insoluble
No pain too inconsolable

This is the grace poured out upon me
This is the foundation, keeping me standing
The truth keeping me from despair
The Word keeping me hoping

I shall not die, but I shall live

"Oh Jerusalem"
(Luke 13:34)

Oh the depths of the passionate love of God
Still driving Him today
Calling out to a lost generation

We are a blinded world
Scrabbling so hard to do it on our own
That we cannot see the Father's broken heart
Bleeding sorrow and forgiveness

We are so preoccupied with our pain
We are oblivious to Jesus' cry of agony
As He pours out His Blood for us

We are focussed on everybody else's faults and
failings
We cannot see the necrotic state of our hearts
And the Gatherer who hangs nailed to a wooden
Cross
Till His earthly life departs
And thus, brings us to Himself

We are so concentrated
On filling our yawning lives with self-righteousness
We cannot see the only Righteous One
Blazing love and glory and freedom from the Throne

And one day it will be too late

"So Run To Win"
(1 Corinthians 9:24)

Prayer is part of the training to run the race …

At the beginning of the day
In the cool chill of the dawn
I stand at the starting post
Talking over the day with my Father

It seems a long haul
The running track stretches out into infinity
Oh God, help me

But my Coach, my Trainer, my Teacher, my Instructor
Puts His arm round me and prepares me
We look at the Training Manual together
He tells me what to expect
How to deal with it
He reminds me that His Son has done the run already
There are no unknowns, no impossibles

Then He pours a measure of His power and strength
and grace
Compressed in a way that is beyond my
comprehension
Into my very heart
"This is my Spirit
This is me, with you
Though you cannot see Me
You will not be alone in the race"
And He gives me the wine of His love to sustain me

As I flex my muscles
Assure Him of my trust and obedience
He whispers the greatest promise of all
"This is but a training day
Your name is already chalked up on the champions'
board
The Lamb has marked you out as one who is coming
home
So go!   Run to win!"

"Long Ago I Ordained It"
(2 Kings 19:25)

I am not your seer, your prophet
I am not going to tell you of your future

It is not for you to seek and strive
To search for that which is not for you to know
Neither is it for you to strain for knowledge and
understanding
It is not profitable or necessary for you

In seeking Me to know Me alone
You will be satisfied
You will find you do not need the answer
You will only need Me

Know this
I am the God of your past
The God of your present
The God of your future
It is I, the King of Kings and the Lord of Lords
Who planned this day

At the time I appoint
I reveal to you My plans
At the hour I appoint I give you My word
Tell you where to go, what to say

It is for you to wait, to worship, to trust

Daily I am moulding your heart
Melding it with Mine
My beloved, do not fear

THE
SEASON OF
QUESTIONS

Why Did You Not Intervene?

Why God?
Why do You not do something?
Still today I continue to ask
Why do You not intervene?

People are abused, forgotten, misunderstood
Become friendless, jobless, penniless
Suffer pain, endure illness, die….

But I see that once
For the love of me
You did not intervene
Your Son was wounded by lashes
Your heart was broken at His death
But You did not intervene

The angels wept
The demons laughed
Your children jeered
But You did not intervene

This is the greatest non-intervention ever known
Bringing victory over death
Eternal life

Oh, praise Him

When?

When will I wake up?
When will we wake up?
Do we really think that anything we have on earth has
any value?
When heaven is the whole purpose of our journey?
Why do we worry about the outer appearance?
The so-called social respectability of a job, a family, a
steady income

When will I wake up?
When will we wake up?
Are we playing an act in a film?
Courting the praise of popular people
Basking in the limelight of flattery
Do we realise that this way will come to an end?
The Judge will call us to account
And the sky will go dark forever

When will I wake up?
When will we wake up?
Am I ready?
Are we ready?

Why?

Why did You do it, Kingly One?
Vacate Your golden throne at the Father's right hand
Leave Your rightful place of majesty where the angels
adore You night and day
Embrace the mantle of mortality

Ache with weariness after a day of travail
Endure fickle friendships, taunts and temptations
Crushed by crowds, yet alone in the Garden

Why did You do it, eternal Son of God?
Allow man to curse You, bind You, kill You
Father's face hidden from view
Facing hell's fury alone

Why?

You did it to smash Satan's stronghold
To break death's grip and rise again
Father, Son and Spirit gloriously reunited
Heaven rejoicing at Your royal return
Your children running to You
Shouting for joy
That is why

Why Do I Believe
In You, Jesus?

Why do I believe in You, Jesus?
What is it about You that makes me believe?
I can't see You or hear You
Touch You, hug You, kiss You

You allow things to happen to me
That fill me with anxiety and sadness
My friends go through trials
Whilst I watch, feeling quite helpless
People everywhere hurt and abuse one another
Some to the point of death

I ask You
What keeps me believing in You?
Believing that You really are there

Why is that I keep coming back to You?
Why do I find earthly pleasures do not satisfy?
Why is it that I don't really enjoy it
When I lie, cheat and envy?

What is it about You that keeps me going?
When the circumstances urge me to run a mile?
What is it about You, Jesus?
You are totally inexplicable

But if I didn't believe
I would be dead
For You see it all
You rip me wide open
You make me alive

Why Do I Believe
In You Jesus? (2)

Why do I believe?
Because I have tasted of the fruit of Your love
Because I can't see anything but You, Jesus

I see You on Your Throne
Hear Your laughter in the silence
Your voice through the clamour
Sense Your stillness in the storm
Receive vision in the darkness

Why do I believe in You, Jesus?
Because there isn't anything else, anyone else

THE
SEASON OF
DARKNESS

How Long?

I live in silence amongst the crowds
I can only bear them for a while
I open my mouth and speak words
But my heart remains closed

The day dawns and I awake
But my soul lies asleep within
I walk, I work, I eat, I sleep
In a cloud

I am a wounded animal
Once proud and strong
Now a shadow
I lie within, inert under crushing pain

How long, Lord, how long?
How long must I creep quietly?
Seeking to evade my hidden agony
Sliding in and out
Avoiding the arrows
Afraid of facing today
Facing the love of You and my friends
Facing myself....

It has been so long
Since I knew Your sun
I am weak with pain
Licking my wounds helplessly
I wait
How long?

Come with Your Spirit
That Spirit that raised Your Son
Do what only You can
I would like to live again

Dead Leaves

I walk in the woods
On a path, obliterated by leaves
Dead leaves

Beneath my feet
The only sound is the crunching of dead leaves
All I can see is dead leaves

I am tired of this merry-go-round life of dead leaves

Lord, bring me out of the pain
Into the sunlight

Meaningless Life

It's all pointless
Life is without meaning

Feelings are so dark and bad
I shut them out
I hate the night, the cold
I don't live in a house
I live in a prison
From which I cannot escape

I do not know how to live
I no longer know the meaning of the word

Am I just covering the cracks?
Dutifully praising, praying and petitioning
When inside I'm dying

Days are spent existing
Where are You Lord?
Why have You allowed this?
When is it going to end?
Hear my anguished cry
A cry from a heart that cannot break free
I am stifled
I cannot do this on my own

I cannot endure it anymore
This never-ending pain

Do You really hear me Lord?
Amid the cacophony of a billion wounded souls?
Can You hear me?

Help me to remember Your kindness
Evidences of Your past presence
Don't let my faith putrefy
Rather let it purify
Don't let me go

Where Are You?

Hear my cry, oh Lord
Hear my cry

Hear the cry of a heart that has known You
That does know You
That has loved You
That does love You

Yet I am wounded and baffled
Confused and angry
Uncertain and afraid

This is my spirit
Crying out to its Maker
This is Your adopted child
Calling out to its Father
This is Your beloved
Seeking out its Lover
Where are You?

In this whirlwind
I can't find You
I stand still
Unable to think, to see
Sensing Your Presence
But it is not enough

Where are You?
Come to me

Loneliness

I am invisible
A non-person
I do not exist
I am a name without a face
A face without a name

At home there is only me
I do not create noise
I hear my neighbour's noise
Therefore, I do not exist
For my home does not exist
I am not there

I am not known
Not as a person
I am lost
I have no life of my own
I do not speak or act or think on my own

I cannot find myself
The past has gone
I cannot find myself today
My dreams are peopled with the past
For there is no present
I love to be with the people of my dreams
But I dread the waking

I meet people when I go out
I switch on
The button is pressed
I speak, I laugh, I listen and I pray
I leave
The light switches off
I no longer exist

I would like to be alive
But I do not know how
I have no interest in hobbies
They give me no pleasure
Who will see them, hear them?
Somewhere inside of me is the person who loved
them
But she is asleep and isn't able to wake up
Until she does, I will be a non-person

I pray

If Jesus didn't weep with me
I don't know where I would be
This is the only place I feel some sense of stability, life,
safety
It's the only place I feel alive

Surviving

It's closing in on me again, Lord
Claustrophobic isolation
Crippling loneliness
Living in a bubble
Everybody, everything else outside

I have retreated behind the glass because I hurt
Tired out, I curl up

All energy is expended
In the effort to survive the day
Nothing is left over
There is nothing to give
I do not know the way out
And I do not know the way ahead

Within the glass bubble
By moving slowly
I avoid overtaking myself
Or banging against brick walls

I breathe in gently, carefully
Hold myself together for a moment
Then quietly, so painfully breathe out again

Living in the silence of me
It is enough to keep life and limb together
Against the clamouring needs of the people who
demand

To me this is agonising, without end

And to You Lord?
Not, it is not so
You are with me
All the time
Every step
Every thought
Every breath

Less and less it seems
Do I know the way
But in the darkness Your light leads me
I only have You, my Lord

In The Fire

He is in the fire
He is the Fire
A Fire that chastens
That I may come forth as gold

I am on fire with loneliness and loss
Within such a Fire I am honed
I am kept safe
I am not alone

In the blazing Fire
I am faced by my self
That has kicked against His light
Within His Fire I find
I no longer want to resist

It is a Fire that burns with His love
It hurts
But to be in the Fire
Is to be with Him, within Him
Never alone
Never

In The Forest

Is it spring?
The trees are still quite bare
But the wood is alive with sound
I am alive in Jesus
Though living in a barren land

In A Dark Place

This is a dark place
The crashing of my dreams and security
Terrible uncertainty

Creeping slowly
Through days of dread and fog
Shutting my eyes and ears against hurt
Blurred thoughts, a dazed mind

I can be strong in my weakness
I can be confident in my fears
For the King is here
Within me
Overcoming, undertaking

It is no longer I that lives but Christ who lives in me

Jesus replies:

In The Desert

I bring you to places where you will meet with me
Deep in the wild, the desert, the dark

I bring you to places where I will speak to you
In the midst of your fears, your pain, your despair,
your dreams

I bring you to places where I will guide you
Out of the world's falsehood and self's condemnation
Into My heart

I bring you to places of the unknown and the
uncertain
Where you will see and hear what you do not
understand
But where you will worship with deep joy
Because I am there

My desire, my little one
Is to bring you to Me

In The Wilderness

Sometimes I take you away into the wilderness
Where there are no footholds
There is no lamplight, no sound
Sometimes I take you to these places
So that your only anchor is Me, Jesus

Sometimes I take you away
To where earth and its passions are of no help or
comfort
To where you are stripped of all you hold dear
And your sole warmth and protection is Me, Jesus

I do this to purify and cleanse and scour
All that has held you, marred you
Sometimes it is the only way

When you come through the darkness
And you will
You will know My love in greater measure
You will find you love Me more than before
This wilderness is My work
Do not be afraid

THE SEASON OF HIS OF HIS PRESENCE

Here

He is here
With the power to perform miracles
The peace to calm every storm
The Creator who formed the stars
The Consoler who captures my tears
He is here

Your Time, Your Day

This is Your time
Where no demon dares enter
Where I am silent

This is Your day
Where you speak and I listen
You direct and I bow
You command and I surrender

This is Your time, Your day
Always
In the quiet and the clamour
You permit life and I breathe
Pour out grace, I revive
Correct a path, I turn
Touch wrongdoing, I confess
Bestow kindness, I sing

This is all Your day and all Your time
Not for me to know my day and my time
Sufficient I embrace Your day and Your time
You
Now
Jesus

Majesty

Majesty, oh Majesty
Crown of life to me
You are honey, You are wine
My morning radiance
My evening glory
Majesty, oh Majesty
You are all to me

Praise Him, oh praise Him
My true Redeemer
Keeper of my heart
Cherisher, Refiner
Fount of sweet delights

Let me press in close
Know Your Lover's kiss
Be consumed by You
For You are all to me

This Is My Song

This is where I begin my song
And this is where it will end
As long as I have breath
In the secret place
Alone and unseen
With You, my Lord

This is where I draw breath
Where I feed
Where I am strengthened
Where I see the Truth

Satan's curse lies broken
My feet stand strong
My hands reach out
My heart leaps

What is the source of my song?
Jesus
For in Him I live

Hidden In Your Love

Opening me up
Calming me
Enveloping me
Stilling my rushing panic
Understanding me without need of words
Confronting me
In Your full intensity
A safe place
A pillow where I can cry
Lost in You
Hidden in Your love, Lord

Just This Moment

Just this moment, Lord
This moment with You
Breathing You in
Savouring You

A touch from Your hand
Your grace
Pouring over me
Sufficient for me
Sheltering me from cruel darts

Just this moment
Enough
Always
Now

Just this moment
With You

Lifted

His scarred hand tilts up my chin
I gaze into eyes that have loved beyond reason
That have borne sorrows beyond knowing

I am loved
At cost beyond price
Drawing the heart of me into His own

True Worship

How can one hour, one minute
One precious pause
In life's headlong rush
Do justice to honouring the King?

How can it be enough?
To express glory to the King of Universe?
How can it be expected His praise can be numbered?
In finite time, with mortal voice?
It cannot

But a sigh from a broken spirit
Brings greater joy to His heart than all of these
Ah, Jesus ....

When I Worship

When I worship
With empty hands
Fractured heart
I see You

When You come to me
Mysteriously
As no other comes to me
When You are there
When it seemed for so long as if You were not
When I see You

Your pierced hands and feet
Your marred face
Your scarred body

I worship
And I am made whole
I am no longer afraid
Ah, breath and hope to me
God of all my desiring

The Source Of Life

My peace comes from praising
My strength from resting
My satisfaction from serving
I will not fear

Perfect Love

Powerful love that holds me
Persistent love that pursues me

You brighten my darkness
Melt my hardness
Still my trembling
Sustain me when strength is gone

When I can't go any further
It is then that You come to me
Again and again
Oh perfect love
I worship You Jesus

My Mercy Song

You are my mercy song
Through the watches of the night
As my parched heart cries out for You
Healing streams of love flow from Your Throne
You are my mercy song

Drops of blood
Pouring over me
The jewels of Your crown
Sacrificial love that tore You from Father's arms
My mercy song

I worship You

I Belong To Him

I have no rights
I am His to command
I live or die according to His will
I prosper or fade as He sees fit
I am His slave
He is my King
His voice I obey
To His word I surrender

His hand feeds me
His mantle covers me
Shields me, protects me, draws me
Into His warmth

It is very simple
It is very wonderful
He is the Lover of my soul
No other
I belong to Him
King Jesus

Walking In Your Shadow

Let me walk in Your shadow dear Jesus
Find shelter in the shade of Your grace
Walk so close I feel the heat of Your presence
I desire to be Your handmaid
The adoring slave lifting up Your train

Oh, to be in Your shadow, dear Jesus
Walking where You walk
Seeing, hearing, feeling what You do
So intimate are our steps
To hear the slightest whisper in my ear
Your breath on my cheek

To wait on You
As I wait upon others
Receiving every rebuke and rejection
As borne for You
That in giving out
I give unto You
That in losing out
I gain reward
Simply by walking in Your shadow, dear Jesus

Becoming Like Him

As I meet with my Saviour
As I walk with Him
I become more like Him
I transform into His likeness
The likeness of life lived under the Cross

Outstretched arms loving a little more
Flesh subdued through willing obedience
Heart crying out for God's wine of grace to fall upon
mankind

As I meet with my Saviour
I become more like Him
I am alive as never before

THE
SEASON OF
JOY

Declare Him

As You silence my tongue...at last
Dear Spirit of the living God, rise up within me
Let heart meet heart in lover's embrace
Now dear Spirit, now

You have waited for opportunity
Opportunity I give to You as I surrender
I bow low that You may be raised high

Let me confess that You are Lord
Yes, You are Lord, You are Lord, You are Lord!
Heart and flesh may fail
But God is the strength of my life and my portion
forever

Truth cries out
Truth burns to be revealed
He is Lord, the glorious Overcomer
He is the Lamb
The Shepherd to the nations
Declare Him, my soul, declare Him

He rides in victory
Standing on the Scorpion's head
Crushing him with glorious cry
Majesty vanquishes death
Truth scatters lies
Joy banishes terror

Declare Him, my soul, declare Him
Seek not to understand
Seek only His glory
Seek only to worship
Come out, come out
From your self-imposed tomb
Come out
For He Himself has come to you

Another Day

This is not just another day
This is the gift of another day
From the Lord

This is a guilt-free day
A day of thankfulness and worship
Of release and hope
A strength-filled, joy-filled day
This is the day that He has made

This is a day of holiness
Separated from idols
United with the Lamb
A day of learning obedience
Growing in wisdom
A day of listening, talking and walking
With the Companion of my soul

This is the day of the Lord
Bringing in His Kingdom
Revealing His Kingdom
Serving His Kingdom
This is His day

This is NOT just another day

Seasons

Thank You for the seasons, Lord
The beauty of creation's seasons
And the seasons of my soul

Thank You for the springtime Lord
Sweet smelling grass, blue skies
Birdsong and blossom
Thank You for the springtimes in my life
The joy of Your presence
The assurance of salvation
The wonder of Your love and grace
Dancing free and forgiven

Thank You for the summertime Lord
Long days, warm evenings
Cloudless skies and sunshine
Thank You for the summertimes in my life
Drinking of the Spirit's power
Feeding, growing in Your Word
Passionate intimate prayer
A fulfilled and contented heart

Thank You for the autumntime Lord
Falling leaves, foggy nights
Colours, lights, shades
Thank You for the autumntimes in my life
Answered prayer, unforeseen trouble
Joys, sorrows, boredom, excitement
Desires fulfilled, dreams denied
Learning to stand, growing in faith

Thank You for the wintertime Lord
Cold mornings, dark nights
Storms, ice, death
Thank You for the wintertimes in my life
An anguished wounded heart
Brokenness, darkness
Silence in my spirit
Transformed under the Refiner's fire

Thank You for the seasons Lord
The seasons of my soul
And through it all
Your eternal, endless grace
Your sustaining, enduring love
Bringing me safely home.

I Dance To A Different Tune

I dance to a different tune
For I have heard the Shepherd's call
The grave is empty
The Cross is bare
Vacated by its royal Prisoner
For He is seated on the Throne of Heaven

I dance to a different tune
Gone the constricting walls of my existence
Traps and snares that caught and wounded me
My past is gone
My old nature is buried
Heaven's Gate is open unto me

I dance to a tune that beats out irresistible life and joy
Breathing the Saviour's hope
To a lost world's agony

I dance a tune that lifts Jesus' Holy Name
Nailing me daily to His Cross
I dance a tune that leads me above my own desires
Into sacrificial service to others

I dance a tune that leads me up the bridal aisle
To my waiting Groom
Surrounded by angels
Hailing God's victory
I dance to the tune of my Father's heartbeat

Will you join me in the dance?

No Greater Victory

The greatest battle that heaven and hell will ever
know
Was won behind a stone
Within a sealed tomb
In a silent, deserted garden

There is no greater victory

In heaven
There are a multitude of saints
Adoring their living Lord
The Son of God
Risen and alive - today

He who was a Jew
Known to a few
Admired by some
Hated by many
This man, this God, this Jesus,
Will one day be the Name on every tongue
Spoken in terror or in joy

There is no greater victory

The Lamb's pierced hands speak the triumph
Life overcoming death
Love bringing in the Kingdom that will never end

There is no greater victory
Remember Him and adore

Jesus The Passover Lamb

Dear Lord Jesus
Thank You that my sin is passed over, removed,
excised
Thank You for being my Passover Lamb
The only acceptable sacrifice

Oh Jesus, the joy of it
All that I once was – gone
Delivered from a fruitless, powerless existence
Made new
Because of You
My Passover Lamb
This is glorious

How impossible and inconceivable
To think of living, breathing without you

I feast on the sweetness, the richness, the purity
Of the bread of the Passover Lamb
This is sufficiency for me
I worship You

God Speaks

God speaks
Rich are His words
Sweet, deep and cleansing
Precious, more precious than gold

No longer breathing out judgement
The fire of death
But the promise of life
For every hungry heart that will believe

How does He do it?
The Eternal God
Reaching into our silence
And speaking life…..

Through an autumn leaf
A child's laugh
A sunbeam
A wise man's eyes

What does He speak?
This Creator and Father
He speaks of His Son, His Chosen One
The perfect Sacrifice

Is this not enough
To make us whole?
To silence trembling fears?
To bring hope, renewal and release?
When God speaks

Jesus Breaks
The Rod

Jesus is our wonderful refuge

When we run to Him
Pleading the Blood
The power of the Cross
Crying out for the covering grace
He breaks the rod

Jesus breaks the rod
That subjects us
To a cycle of self-condemnation and penance

Jesus breaks the rod
That iron grip on our lives
Bending us double
Constricting us
Suffocating us
With guilt, pain, helplessness, failure, fear, shame

Jesus breaks the rod
That has had us staggering drunkenly under its
oppressive weight
Lurching uncertainly from one crisis to another

Hope to despair, joy to disappointment
Faith to doubt, trust to anger

Jesus breaks the rod
That assails us with accusation
Deceiving us
Crushing us into a hardened ball
Of self-rejection, hopelessness
Defiance, disobedience

Jesus breaks the rod
Bearing the rod of punishment for us
Rising gloriously, victoriously
Providing a canopy of shelter
Stretching out endlessly
Jesus has broken the rod
Jesus breaks the rod

I Am Free

You have set my spirit free
I can dance
You have lifted the heaviness
I am light
I can fly

This body has been weighted with stones
This mind has been clouded with pain
This heart has been locked fast
But I am released
I am free

Free is the word, Lord
Free to sing and dance and laugh
No longer acting out my part
A puppet on a string

Free to be me
Free to be the me I am in You
Free to share me
Free to share You
Free to speak without fear
Free to work, to rest, to serve
Without restraint

In dark places You have shepherded
Laid your hand heavy upon me
Here I stay
Forever broken, lamed
Forever Yours

By breaking me
You are making me whole
Healing my broken heart.
And making me new in You
I am free

I Can See Your Face

You have taken away my disgrace
I can see Your face
You have removed the veil from my face
That suffocated my heart

You have clothed me in Your beauty
Filled me with peace
No more disgrace
I can see Your face

The shame is gone
The promise has come
No longer abandoned, forsaken
Forgotten, rejected

I live unafraid and untroubled
Reconciled, accepted
Desired, loved by You

You have taken away my disgrace
I can see Your face
I am Yours

Uncontainable God

The bottle has been uncorked
God's fragrance has spilled out
The fragrance of His grace

Uncontainable God has been poured out
Through the love-blood of the Son
Undeserved mercy
Flowing free

God and His grace cannot be restrained
He saturates, He permeates
There is no going back
For Him or for man
He rules, He conquers
He will complete the work He has begun
Fulfilling all His promises
He will have His way

It Is He

It is He that causes me to stand

For it is His Hand that holds me
His Arm that strengthens me
His Heart that emboldens me

It is He that gives me hope
Saves me through fires of fear
Guides me through the dark night
Arms me in the onslaught, the blood of battle
Whispers words in the cold alone
Shouts for joy in my pleasures
It is Jesus, only Jesus
Wonderful, wonderful Jesus
I am His living witness

Yours

Yours is the day
And Yours is the night
Yours is the salvation
And Yours the redemption
Yours the keys to life
Yours the gates of death
Yours and Yours alone

Yours are the hands that hold
That raise up
And cast down
That provide and withhold
Yours and Yours alone

Yours is the voice that speaks
Yours the voice that shakes the earth
Yours is the command
Yours the authority
Yours and Yours alone

Yours is the breath that caresses
Yours the heat of fire
Yours is the power that shatters shackles
The might that destroys demons
Yours and Yours alone

Yours is the glory
The honour, the majesty, the dominion
Yours is the strength
The triumph and the victory
Yours and Yours alone
King Jesus!

He Alone

Sometimes
When I pray
I open my eyes
Expecting to see Jesus there
So near does He feel

He alone is the One I fear and reverence
Yet He alone in all of the heaven and earth
Is the One with whom I have the most intimate
relationship
My Lord

He alone understands me, loves me
Convicts me and pardons me
Pursues me, captures me
Laughs with me
Cries with me

He alone gives life
Creates and controls
He alone drives breath in, then out
Causes eyes to blink, skin to sweat, voice to sing
Blood to pulse, heart to beat
He alone gives free will to express emotions
To make decisions and choices

He alone allows wounds
And He alone pours out healing oil

He alone of His great graciousness does this

He alone is always there in every place all the time
He alone
My Jesus

He Alone (2)

He alone and always Him alone
Brother, Friend, Lover, Husband, Bridegroom
Servant, Master, Captain, Saviour, King
Beginning and End
He alone

He alone is the one that pours out fountains of praise
from our pens
And streams of song from our spirits
He alone can do it

He alone is triumphant in the heavens
He alone has mighty host of angels singing
never-ending praise
He alone sits on golden throne
With incense of the saints' prayers infusing the holy
air
He alone
And then He alone is preparing thrones for His
children!
Glorious, glorious God

He alone delivers us out of the hands of our enemies
His Blood alone cleanses, His Cross alone raises
He alone holds Satan's time in His hands

Demolishing demons at a breath
Strongholds at a glance

He alone is worthy of all that we have
And all that we are
He alone and only Him shall have all
He alone has called us to Himself
He shall in no way turn us away
He alone is God, our God, our wonderful God
Our Jesus, our Jesus

He Alone (3)

He alone hides me in the high place
Covers me, keeps me, shields me
As the apple of His eye
He alone watches over me in the darkness of the night
Hears every whispered sigh and shout of joy
He alone

He alone is faithful
Trustworthy and true
He alone knows my tomorrow
Hides it from my gaze
And He alone opens up my today
According to His sovereign will

He alone who was there when I was birthed
Will meet me at life's end

He alone will I serve and worship for all eternity
Most holy God

THE
SEASON OF
EXPECTATION

Take Me To The Place

Lord, take me to that place where night never darkens
the sky
And the cold never chills the air
Lord, take me to the place where the music never ends
And tears never fall
Lord, take me to the place where leaves never wither
and blooms never fade
Lord take me to the place where souls never weary
and hearts never ache
Lord, take me to the place where You live

I know there is such a place
Sometimes I have blinked and been dazzled by a flash
of it
My finger tips have brushed the door frame
Have been seared by the touch
And my ears have heard the refrain of a song
Sweeter than that of any nightingale
Lord, take me to that place

Getting Ready

When I cry again
"How long to the marriage, my Lord, my Lamb?"
I rest, content with Your reply
I love the silence which You fill
And with which You fill me

Then I cannot add anything by word or action to Your
perfection
I have no question, no demand, no complaint of You
There is no more from me
Just more, and more of You

"For the wedding of the Lamb has come, and His
bride has made herself ready"

One Day

One day the waiting will be over, Lord
One day
One day there will be no more wrestling with anxious
thoughts
And an end to endless silent weeping
Final victory against evil

One day I shall see You as You really are Lord
And I shall see myself!
I will be in a forever heart embrace
One day

One day it will be more than just glimpses
An occasional touch from heaven
Flashes of joy
One day

Oh the longing, the wondering, the waiting
For that One Day
But for now
I am silent, secure, surrendered
For I see Your outstretched arms
Ready to greet me
One day

We Are One

We feel isolated by grief and loneliness
Trapped and imprisoned by our circumstances
Gazing longingly at what others have and we do not
And will never have
We yearn for deep friendships
But are too busy, too apathetic
We mourn over broken relationships
Our lives are torn apart, devastated
Or we face another grey day of boredom, illness,
silence

But this we all have
A oneness in the Son
You are a part of me, and I am a part of You
We are cleansed through the Blood of the Lamb
We are made one through His love
He is one with us
And one day we shall see Him face to face

When Jesus Calls Me

When Jesus calls me
When the trumpet sounds
There will be a place for me
Prepared for me
Right for me
Judged fitting for me

There will be open doors
Windows through which the sun always shines
Gates to wide pastures

There I shall see those all those I have ever known
And others besides
These also shall I know

One shall know another as never before
One shall be one with another
No need of talk or explanation
All will be known
We shall see and move and live in one another
In pure holiness and joy
Our speech will be of things not known on earth

What was sung through the veil
Will become praise, triumphant and complete
There will be union between all
And joy
One shall be one with another, two others
Ten others, a hundred others, a thousand, a million
Yet one never the same as another

When Jesus calls me
When the trumpet sounds

When Jesus Calls Me (2)

When Jesus calls me
When the trumpet sounds
I will never be sad again
Death will be swallowed up in victory

I will sing
Not by an act of my will, or on command
But because I will see Jesus
It will not be possible to cease my praise
The new body I will receive
Will never stop its song

When Jesus calls me
When the trumpet sounds

When Jesus Calls Me (3)

When Jesus calls me
When the trumpet sounds
I will meet my Lord
What Spirit has whispered as the truth
Will be truth indeed

The day of battle will be over
Forever I shall be His
I shall know it
See it, feel it, live it, rejoice in it

The shadow life will be over
When I take my last earthly breath
Eternity will begin
When I meet with my Lord
When Jesus calls me
When the trumpet sounds

When Jesus Calls Me (4)

Today's troubles, trials and anxieties are nothing
Nothing compared to what is to come
What is being prepared for me
What is already there
All the stillness
All the laughter
All the beauty
That I have known – so fleetingly
So imperfectly, so longingly
I will know in entirety, in depth, in glory

Beyond earth's eye
I will rest
Rest in my Lord's arms
Alive as never before

When Jesus calls me
When the trumpet sounds

The Lord Is Coming

The Lord, the Lord is coming
Hear His Wind among the tree tops
The Lord, the Lord is coming
His Kingdom is upon us
His glory is appearing
His day is very near
The Lord, the Lord is coming

Open wide your gates
Open up your hearts
To the searing of His holy Flame
Branding us with pure grace

The Lord, He is visiting us
Reach out and touch Him
As He passes by
He is feeding hungry hearts
Embracing wounded souls
The Lord, the Lord is coming among us

Open wide your gates
Open up your hearts
Prepare a pathway
That the people may see the matchless King
The Lord, the Lord is coming
The Lord day's is very near